I Won't Give Up

Unlock The Treasures Waiting For You

Kay Stephens

ENTEGRITY
CHOICE PUBLISHING

Entegrity Choice Publishing
PO Box 453
Powder Springs, GA 30127
info@entegritypublishing.com
www.entegritypublishing.com
770.727.6517

Printed in the United States of America

All scriptures are from the New King James Version Bible.

Library of Congress Cataloging-in-Publication Data
ISBN 978-1-7325767-7-3
Library of Congress Control Number: 2018966775

For everyone who thought about giving up, continue on your journey and reach the rainbow, so you can enjoy the treasures.

Acknowledgements

To my parents and my family: You have given more of yourselves than imaginable. I thank you for tremendous amount of love, support, and encouragement. Thank you for allowing me to experience life to the fullest without boundaries. Thank you for not giving up on me.

To my friends and peers: Most of what I learned in life is from you. We all have a special part to play in this world and it the lives on the people we come into contact with and we should make the most out of every opportunity. Our time together is priceless. Thank you for the memories.

A very special thank you to all Pastors, who have placed their belief and trust in God. Thank you for allowing God to use you to spread the Gospel. Thank you for your willingness to share with me (Doctor Arthur Carson Jr., Pastor Dave Divine, Pastor Donald Bryant, Pastor Bettye Holland-Williams and Pastor Jasper Williams Jr.).

Contents

Introduction

To My Dear Friends,

Every human being at one time or another has thought about giving up. Has the thought ever crossed your mind? You are not alone; the thought has crossed my mind. This book is an awakening to the life you have and the life you have yet to experience. Please stop whatever your mind is telling you and read this book. It will open your eyes to what lies ahead while unlocking what God has for you.

I press on toward the goal to win the prize for which God has called me heavenward in Christ Jesus. (Philippians 3:14)

I am writing this book, not because of something I have read, but because of things I have experienced in life. I am not a therapist or a psychologist. These are simply tried and true methods that have worked for me over and over again, and I pray that they will work for you. God has created miracles in my life that I would not have had the opportunity to experience, if I were dead spiritually or physically.

I believe that you want to live life to the fullest because you are reading this book. Maybe you received this book from someone who cares about you very much and wants you to live and have a bright and successful future.

Whatever the reasons, since you have the book, you have nothing to lose. Give it a try! Read it. Follow the exercises before you make any other decisions. Start living a life of contentment, today, a life of handling everyday challenges with divine favor from God. Then watch God create miracles in your life. You hold the keys to live life to the fullest. I wish you the very best on your journey.

To God be the Glory,

Kay

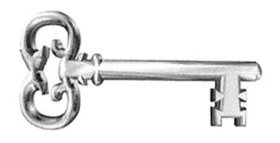

Action is the foundational key
to all success.

-Pablo Picasso

1

Stopping

Stopping the pain. Pain comes from a variety of sources-sickness, injury, stress, worry, or the loss of a loved one. Pain can even come from living with a medical condition or from surviving an accident. The Mayo Clinic, which is the largest medical facility in the world, has confirmed that stress can cause pain. By eliminating stress you are stopping the pain.

Unhealthy stress can limit one's ability to function day to day. Just getting out of the bed and doing daily routines can cause a frustrating feeling of sadness and cause one to ask the question: what's the point? Why do I have to do this? Unhealthy stress causes depression, mood swings, sadness, anxiety, negative attitudes, negative behavior and can continue to interrupt your day.

When you are experiencing unhealthy stress, daily routines can seem like major tasks. Stress can come from your job, your school, your own state of mind, as well as from relationships with family members, friends, associates, bosses and teachers. We live in a world that promotes perfection. Most people want to satisfy others, i.e., looking good for others and doing well for others. Society leads us to believe that if you have lots of money, a nice car, a big house and an attractive companion, then you are succeeding in life. This is not true at all!

Success is how you define it and why it is important to you. When you don't meet the world's definition of success, you feel like a failure, and this often leads to unhealthy stress and pain.

You intended to harm me, but God intended it for good to accomplish what is now being done…(Genesis 50:20)

Stop believing what the commercials are selling you. Your body and your brain are connected and are in constant communication with each other sending messages, and if you are experiencing unhealthy stress, you are receiving messages of pain. Where there is a high level of unhealthy stress, there is pain. Not being free from stress and pain, can make some people feel like giving up. What's most important at this moment is that you are aware of your pain and the need to make it go away.

Mind-body advocates contend that you have more power over your pain than you realize. Once you recognize that there is pain in your life, you have to find a way to stop or numb the pain. It is important to stop or numb the pain because you cannot experience the life that you desire living, feeling pain every day.

Many turn to drugs, legal and illegal, to ease their pain. It has been proven that illegal drugs, alcohol and self-destructive addictions do not help, but destroy your chances of stopping the pain. The U.S. National Library of Medicine National Institutes of Health states that each year drug abuse results in around 40 million serious illnesses or injuries among people in the United States.

Drug abuse also plays a role in many major social problems, such as drunk driving, violence, stress and child abuse. Drug abuse can lead to homelessness, crime, missed days at work or school, or problems with keeping a job. It harms unborn babies and destroys families. Alcohol and self-destructive addictions can impact you the same way as drugs. There are other ways to stop the pain of stress without throwing in the towel. You can learn to have control over pain.

Over the past few decades, research has verified that mind–body therapies may help eliminate various types of pain and prevent its recurrence. Techniques that were once considered complementary or alternative, such as, behavioral therapy, biofeedback, cognitive therapy, guided/ visual imagery, hypnosis, meditation, and relaxation therapy have become the main focus today.

The pain may not stop completely, but it can be "numbed" to the point where you are able to continue without feeling the stress, pressure, embarrassment or the loss of hope. Researchers have conferred that pain is a mental state. If you think you can stop the pain, guess what, you can. If you think you cannot stop the pain, guess what, you cannot. Learning to control your mind to ease or stop the pain is not a problem; there are professionals who can help you.

A study has shown that pain treatments and alternative treatment programs that use mind–body interventions have discovered the pain signals and have redirected the signals to send healthy messages to the brain (Wahbeh, Elsas, Oken, 2010). Some of the feelings we have, such as feelings of anxiety, tension, anger, or depression, could cause unassociated responses to the brain.

When your brain has to respond to a huge amount of negative stimuli, you are indifferent, unconcerned and insensible. These responses can eventually send pain messages to your body. You may feel as if you have flu symptoms, fatigue, chills, fever, body aches and headaches. Your brain is sending the message to your body that you are sick and your body is responding. Alternative mind-body treatment requires professional help to pin point what is causing the pain.

Many people have considered giving up, and some have actually tried it. There are many things that you would miss seeing or doing if you give up. Why use a permanent solution for a temporary problem? Just imagine never seeing God's work in the form of the Seven Wonders of the World, or never hearing your favorite artist in a concert, or tasting or smelling new and delicious food for the first time. Imagine the experience of watching Niagara Falls as the water splashes on you, and you later discover that you look like a wet cat, just by being near it. Those things are only a small sample of what the world has to offer and what you would be giving up. It is easy to quit, but if you stick with it, God has something special and unique for you says Dr. Carson.

"Life is a test. It is only a test." You can pass the test with time if you have determination and a course of action. Hang in there.

Trust God with all your heart and lean not to your own understanding; in all your ways submit to him, and he will make your paths straight. (Proverbs 3:5-6)

When the pain stops or numbs, get busy and move on to the next phase of your life.

2

Acceptance

There was pain in your life, but you have stopped or numbed the pain. Right away you have to accept where you are in your life as a focal point. Accepting is important because it helps you to really see the person you are right now, not the person you were yesterday or will be tomorrow. Focusing on yourself is something that you may not have done lately. I want you to really see yourself for the first time in a way you have never pictured yourself before now. By doing this, you will help to bring clarity to who you are and what you are capable of accomplishing.

Get up and dress in your best attire. If

it is a suit, a gown or just your favorite shirt or pants, do it promptly. Look at yourself in a full length mirror and say to yourself, "I accept who I am." Accept your intelligence, your complexion, your body and your race. Next, accept your traits, skills, abilities and your weaknesses. Accept the job you have, accept that you are a student, accept the relationship you are in and accept that you are not the person you used to be or that you wanted to be in your life. Stop reading; do the activity listed above; then continue to read. You may be excellent at drawing but lousy at dancing. That is ok. If you were perfect, you would be God. Do not compare yourself to others. Accept all of yourself and do the best you can with what you have to offer!

Accept the cards that life has dealt you, the decisions that you have made to get to this point, and don't look back.

But (Lot's) wife looked back, and she became a pillar of salt. (Genesis 19:26)

You can dwell on your past tests, guilt, failures, pain and loss, but it does not help you grow into the person that you desire to be in life. I believe Lot's wife died due to her hesitation to remove herself from her situation. Sometimes, we can stay in an unhealthy relationship or an unhealthy state of mind until it kills us physically, spiritually and emotionally. Don't allow past troubles to engulf you; start focusing on your future. It does not matter where you have been or where you are in life. What does matter is moving quickly to get to where you want to be in life.

Brothers and sisters, I do not consider myself yet to have taken hold of it. But one thing I do: Forgetting what is behind and straining toward what is ahead. (Philippians 3:13)

Next, be thankful for who you are and all that you have in your life. You may not be who you want to be or you may not have all that you want to have, but don't stop trying. There are many "rags to riches" stories in the world. The main theme in all of the stories is that the person realized he or she had a problem, accepted it and did something about it. Be thankful for what God has blessed you with in life and don't dwell on what you don't have in life.

Give thanks in all circumstances; for this is God's will for you in Christ Jesus.
(1 Thessalonians 5:18)

Once you have done that, you can start working on living and living life to the fullest. If you have accepted who you are at this point in your life; say to yourself, "I am here at this point in my life, and I need to make some changes in order to have changes in my life." Now, visualize what you need to get rid of in your life in order to become the person you desire.

You know what you need to do, so begin today to eliminate negative thoughts, negative people, negative behavior and negative beliefs from your life. Remove the excess garbage that is holding you back. Write it down. Chances are those things are not what you need or want in your life. No second guessing yourself. Put the trash where it belongs, in the trash can. However, do not take this to the extreme. You don't want to think of yourself more highly than you should. I want you to get to a point in your life, where you will love God first and yourself second. For everyone or everything that has been pulling you down and draining your energy, it is time to give them, or it, an eviction notice.

What a relief it is to finally accept the truth that things are not the way you want them and that you need to do something about it. It should feel as if your cage door has been opened wide and you are now able to lift your arms and fly high above in the skies. You no longer feel weighed down by hopelessness. You feel the joy of hope and the sky is the limit! Ok, come down from the sky for a moment; you still have work to do.

Set a 30-day plan for removing the trash in your life. After 30 days, check your progress. What have you accomplished? If you are still working on it, no problem. Write down what is left to do and do it. Set a deadline to get it done and measure your progress. Don't let it drag out. Once you have disposed of the unneeded items in your life, it is time to celebrate. Always celebrate what you have accomplished. "Celebration time, come on…" Celebration song by Kool & The Gang. This is your life. Don't wait for someone else. Worship, dance or praise the Lord for yourself. Do it as if no one is watching you. Your life is important to you, so celebrate.

Once you have accepted your reality, you will notice that the pain is easier to bear, even if it has not completely disappeared. You can, however move on and do what you need to do to live life to the fullest. You don't have to like where you are in your life, but you do have to come to terms with it and strive to better the situation. You now have a goal and a deadline for getting to the next level. You have created a one-of-a-kind and unique plan for your life. Now you can begin to break down the barriers that have prevented you from having the life you deserve for yourself.

Your Aha Moments

3

Possibilities

Your mind can be a canvas for creating a wonderful, fascinating world filled with a bright rainbow of colors, dreams, hopes and joy. The possibilities are mind-blowing. What possibilities are waiting for you in the future? Let's time travel to a future where you are a millionaire. You have all the resources in the world, and there is nothing blocking your path.

In order to live life to the fullest, it is important to discover everything about what you want to have, do, become or change. You will be amazed at the things you never thought about doing. It is like building a house. When you begin, you may want to look at many different styles in order to select the very best one for your personality. If one style does not meet your satisfaction, you have others to select from. You can add so many features to a house that your list will be amazing. The list of possibilities you will create is like a house.

It is your blueprint to your future life. It will be like a wish list that never stops. Where will you live, what school will you attend, what will you do, where will you work, how will you look and where will you travel? Will you be married and will you have kids? What type of car will you drive and how will your home look? Maybe you should divide the possibility list into categories: Church and Community, Family and Friends, Careers and Businesses, Travel and Other.

Think about the unlimited possibilities that you have in life. Get a sheet of paper and a pen and create a possibility list. Give yourself about 10 minutes to do this. Then close your eyes and think about your possibility list for a moment and how it makes you feel. Can all that you image come true? Sure it can. If you can believe it, you can achieve it.

If you have faith as small as a mustard seed, you can say to this mulberry tree, 'Be uprooted and planted in the sea,' and it will obey you. (Luke 17:6)

Review your possibilities. If you have less than 40 items, keep thinking until you reach 40 items. The number 40 in the Bible is a significant number because it is related to trials, testing, prosperity and probation of God's people.

I can do all things through him who gives me strength. (Philippians 4:13)

Anyone can name a few items and call it a day. I want you to really think about what you want. Write down things you like to do. Think about this time in your life as a self-exploration study. You can take a free on-line assessment to generate jobs you are interested in. Look at different hobbies and entrepreneurship magazines. Think of things that you can sell. Don't think about whether people will buy them; just write them down. Think of things you can do to help someone. Are there things that you can make? What do you really want to have, do, or become?

Remember, if you had no limits and money were not an object, what would you want? What are some of your dreams and wishes? What are some of the things you want to happen in your life? Don't think about what you can't do. This is your list. If everything came true within 24 hours, how would your life change? Don't worry about what you write down. Your list can change and it will change. That's why it is called a "possibilities list".

Once you have reached 40 items, you can stop thinking because you have dug deeply to explore every possible option. Hopefully, you have included in your list this item, "giving back some of your time, talents or treasures to help someone else." You will never experience life to the fullest unless you share what God has given you with others.

Now that you have your blueprint (your possibilities list), you have laid the foundation for your success. No house is ever built without a foundation.

For I know the plans I have for you," declares the Lord, "plans to prosper you and not to harm you, plans to give you hope and a future. (Jeremiah 29:11)

Your foundation is your faith and trust in God. Even before the beginning of the world, God was there and He will always be with you.

Other major components of building a house such as framing, plumbing, installing electrical wiring and insulating, you already possess. In addition to your blueprint, foundation, and other attributes, you have to look at the details inside the house. There has to be balance within your house and within your life. In order to live your life to the fullest, you have to be well-rounded. If you have too much of one thing, something else will be out of balance. Abraham Maslow, an American psychologist, created a theory based on human's needs called the "Hierarchy of Needs." This hierarchy consists of five different needs: (1) Physiological Needs (the need for water, air, food, and sleep). (2) Safety Needs (the need safety and security). (3) Social Needs (the need for belonging, love and affection). (4) Esteem Needs (the need for things that reflect on self-esteem, personal worth, social recognition, and accomplishment). (5) Self-actualizing Needs (the need for self-awareness, concerned with personal growth, less concerned with the opinions of others, and interested in fulfilling their potential).

If I had the liberty to add a sixth need to Masow's list, it would be Medical Needs (the need for medical attention). If you are taking any types of medicine or illegal drugs, or alcohol, or if you are exhibiting extreme behaviors or feeling emotionally drained, please seek professional help. It could not only save your life, but make your life so much better.

Review and revise your possibilities list to include any details you may have omitted from the list above. These are the details that will frame the interior of the house. The bottom line is you can have all the money and no one to love. You can work long and hard and have no one to share it with or leave it to. Don't be Mr. or Mrs. Scrooge. Live, love and share with others.

Hot off the press! You have your catalog of possibilities. You can imagine what life looks like outside of your present four walls. Life is waiting on you to discover it and to test it.

Your Aha Moments

4

Coping

Coping is a process of preparing you for your new lifestyle while attempting to overcome the everyday challenges of life. Take care of your basic needs while you prepare your mind and your environment for the change.

Perform numbers 1 through 6, from what I call Maslow's revised list, before moving on to the pot at the end of the rainbow which is located in Chapter 3.

Sometimes all you need is food and rest. You may need a safe place before you can continue. Whatever your needs are, you must work on them, before you can begin living your life to the fullest. You should carry out your everyday functions by just doing them and not thinking about them. Whatever it is, do it. If you have to work, go to school, go to the doctor, just do it.

If you are unemployed, create a schedule for yourself that will occupy your time the way you wish it could be in the future. Try your very best to get through each day one day at a time. You have to remain calm and patient while coping. Getting upset will be like adding fuel to a fire.

He gives strength to the weary and increases the power of the weak. (Isaiah 40:29)

You will soon realize that there is someone in the world going through the same situation you are going through, if not worst. If you trust God and not worry, things will work out for your benefit.

You have to see it, believe it and be ready to move toward making it happen.

Find what will keep you going everyday and add it to your life. Have something to look forward to when you wake up every morning. Coping mechanisms will vary for everyone. Some people cope by reading motivational stories, watching Oprah's Lifeclass Episodes, SuperSoul Conversations, Pastor Joel Osteen or movies. Others may listen to music, sermons or comedians. Some exercise and some may even sleep. If all else fails, locate a professional with whom you can share your concerns.

Let the peace of Christ rule in your hearts, since as members of one body you were called to peace. And be thankful. (Colossians 3:15)

The only way your life will change is to make the change yourself. If you are unhappy with your present situation (your job, your environment, your friends, family, your health, your school or a relationship), what are you doing about it? Don't focus on what you don't like about your life. Just continue to do your everyday routines, until you can reach the point where you can do something else. If you are just tired of being sick and tired, just continue to hang on.

Keep on doing what you need to do, what you are expected to do, and have to do, until you have a plan. Stop complaining and start doing something about it. You need a plan where you can replace what you are doing with something that will bring you contentment. If a person is holding you back, you must decide the role this person will play in your life 5-10 years down the road. If you do not see a future in that person, then you must make an intelligent decision to do what is best for you.

Enter relationships that are enjoyable and productive for all involved. For example, I was in a bad relationship, and it was making me physically and mentally sick. I stayed until I realized I was not valued in it, so I moved out and ended the relationship. Moving out and ending the relationship made me feel safe and secure. I was able to live my life in a more harmonious ways.

At another time, I was in a job and the job paid all my bills, but I was bored and did not like what I was doing. I felt my job did not give any value to me or anyone else. I just made money for the company. I continued that job until I was able to replace it with a new job. The new job added value to my life and increased my growth.

Negative thoughts and feelings will wear you down to the point where you will not accomplish anything but depression. You must maintain a positive attitude and a positive mindset. Memorize your favorite Bible Verse. One of my favorite verses is Isaiah 26:3.

> *You will keep in perfect peace*
> *those whose minds are steadfast,*
> *because they trust in you.*

When you have a clear mind, with pleasing thoughts, you will work for hours on your possibility plan and not realize what time it is on the clock. Focus on the future and say to yourself, "I have a dream and I won't give up." Bishop T.D. Jakes has a saying, "this is my transportation to my destination." You can always make up your own sayings. These positive statements are called affirmations. They affirm and declare your beliefs.

To find more examples of affirmations, before you write down your affirmation, read books on the subject or search the internet. Write down an affirmation that best describes you, one you will remember and say every day. What you are doing is developing, not only a clear mind, but a pleasant disposition. When things go wrong, and they will, you can recall what you have declared over your life.

Following this, let's prepare your environment. Look at your surroundings.

Let's do some housekeeping. Put up your favorite quotes, words of inspirations, pictures and anything that will inspire you and help you accomplish your goal. Put them up somewhere you will see daily; for example, in the kitchen, in the bathroom and on the doors.

The Lord himself goes before you and will be with you; he will never leave you nor forsake you. Do not be afraid; do not be discouraged. (Deuteronomy 31:8).

If you are still having difficulties with daily routines, start a hobby, write in a journal, join an organization, do meditation, or increase the activities you are currently doing. Start reading more inspirational books, listening to more music, saying more affirmations, and definitely praying more. Sometimes the best recourse is to do nothing at all; just be still and wait.

I have been a member of several organizations (church activities, Girl Scouts,

Boy Scouts, 4H, Kiwanis, ABWA, SHRM, R.I.S.E. and other professional organizations) and have received inspirations by participating. Some of my basic needs were satisfied when I took the time to help and work with others. I discovered that, despite being busy, there are times when I need to be idle. I sit outside on my deck, watch the trees dance with the breeze, and look upward at the clear blue sky.

Do all you can without resorting to any addictions.

No temptation has overtaken you except what is common to mankind. And God is faithful; he will not let you be tempted beyond what you can bear. But when you are tempted, he will also provide a way out so that you can endure it. (1 Corinthians 10:13)

When you are coping with your situation, there will come a point where either the situation will change or you will change your attitude towards the situation.

Remember that job I told you about earlier. Well everyday I went to work grudgingly, wishing I could do something else. I would pray before and during my shifts. I would tell God: see what I have to put up with; this is not worth it. I tried to have a positive attitude, but I constantly thought to myself: this is hopeless. I am going to have to find another job. Then one day, I went to work and the work I was doing had changed. A year later, I had replaced that job with another job. While I was thinking that there was no change in sight, God was behind the scenes working out the details.

Just hang in there until change occurs. Your experience will only make you stronger, if you allow it. Coping is just a detour to your blessing. God has a pre-ordained route to a bright future just for you. It is up to you to seek it out and follow your dreams.

Your Aha Moments

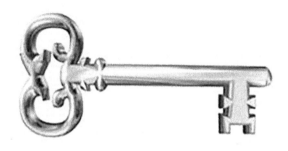

Before anything else,
preparation is the key to success.

-Alexander Graham Bell

5

Adjusting

You have seen what your possibilities look like and you are coping with your current situation. Now imagine the bigger picture so that you can see what a big, bright future you have in store. Your future is like following the yellow brick road to a happy home or finding that pot of gold at the end of the rainbow.

Therefore, if anyone is in Christ, the new creation has come: [a] The old has gone, the new is here. (2 Corinthians 5:17)

You have your list of possibilities. Choose one of the possibilities from your list, and then create an action plan to make it happen. There are many different action plans from simple to complex. One of my favorite action plans was created by Keller Williams Realty. It is called the 4-1-1 Action Goal Worksheet. You can search for a copy on the internet. I still use it today. Another one I like to use is called "Just Do It". I created a worksheet which is listed below. The action plan is simple to complete and will ask you specific questions that will lead you to accomplishing your goal.

You should already have written down the affirmation that best describes you. Revise your affirmation so that it will motivate you to complete your goal on time successfully. Once you are finished, write the revised affirmation on the worksheet or write your favorite Bible verse. Fill in each section and really think about your goal and how you can complete it in the time frame you have listed.

There are people who will be more than willing to help you. Add to your list a person that you don't know, a person whom you would like to meet, or a person you would like to know more about. Write a letter; send an email or a tweet. Contact that person on Facebook or LinkedIn and tell them a little about yourself, your goal and what you are trying to accomplish. Tell the person why meeting the goal is important to you and ask whatever questions you want to know answers to. You will be pleasantly surprised by the answers and what people are willing to share with you.

If you are sincere and have an open mind, you will absorb more. Keep in mind that stalking is not permitted at any time, and it is against the law! If you are not the type of person who wants to contact someone directly or you don't get a favorable reply, then do research about that person. Read and discover everything you want to know to help you accomplish your dreams. I asked to meet with two famous people whom I have admired for a long time, and they were both very kind and receptive as they answered the questions that I had for them. I was told by one, that whatever I do in life, do not have too many people around helping me make decisions. There is an old saying, "too many cooks in the kitchen spoil the broth." The information that was shared with me, I still use today.

Your action plan should cover all areas of your life: Physiological Needs, Security Needs, Social Needs, Esteem Needs, Self-Actualizing Needs, and Medical Needs. Reflect on Maslow's revised list in the Possibilities chapter.

When you start to work on your possibilities, it will feel great because you know that you are working on something that you have decided to do, not something someone else wants you to do, or something you feel obligated to do. You are accomplishing your goal and you will see it through. Just think about it. If you put time into anything, whatever it is, something will come from it. Try to visualize the scene in this familiar saying, "if you shoot for the moon, if you miss, you are still amongst the stars."

Make time to work on your possibilities. Working on your action plan everyday, if possible, is a way to adjust yourself for New Beginnings in life. Once you start working on your action plan, everything else will fall into place to make your possibilities a reality. Write this question down on a piece of paper and place it where you will see it everyday. The question is: "What are you going to do today to make your possibilities come true?" You are almost there, don't give up!

Make your adjustments the "transportation to your destination." You stopped the pain; you have accepted your current life situation; you have your possibilities list; you are coping with daily challenges; and you are adjusting by working towards your goal. Until you see one of your possibilities come true, just wait patiently on the Lord, and He will give you more than you could ever ask for in life. I am a witness. God has blessed me over and over again.

Continue to live day by day the best you can. Strive to motivate yourself until you see your New Beginnings. Prayers to God will keep you focused and allow you to persevere with faith to continue. In brief, these distinguishing features will lead to your future goal and the promises that God has for you. It feels great and refreshing to know that you have a clear visual outlook that you can see even through the fog of life. Be patient with yourself. It will take time and commitment. You must continue to forge ahead and not give up. Forgive yourself when you make mistakes. Have a sense of humor and do not give up.

There are still two important questions to ask yourself: Are you ready for a change, new challenges, new obstacles, and a New Beginning? Or would you prefer to make some temporary adjustments in your life until you are ready? Whatever decision you make, the Action Worksheets will assist you in your journey. The decision is yours!

"JUST DO IT"

My Personal Plan for (Year) _____	Affirmation or Favorite Bible Scriptures
	_____ _____ _____ _____ _____ _____ _____ _____

GOAL: _____

Start Date: _____

Completion Date: _____

Comments about the first 3 to 6 months of your journey:

Comments about the last 7 to 12 months of your journey:

"JUST DO IT"

I want to achieve my goal because:

I will do the following tasks to complete my goal:

I won't be distracted by people, places or things:

I will get support from the following people:

I will motivate myself by doing the following:

I will give back some of my time, talent and treasure to:

Your Aha Moments

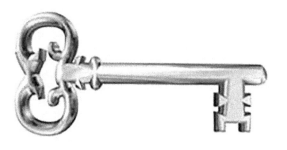

If opportunity doesn't knock,
build a door.

-Milton Berle

6

New Beginnings

Congratulations for making the decision to have a life by your design! The only way you can start your New Beginnings is to openly and honestly list all your possibilities.

If you have not read or completed Chapters 1-6, please stop right now and finish them before going forward.

New Beginnings are just like a married couple being told they are going to have a baby. They are excited and scared at the same time. First, they have to comprehend what they were just told. Next, they have to accept the fact that they are going to have an additional person with them most of the time. Then, they have to prepare for the child financially, physically and mentally. They must make sure the insurance will cover all the cost. Finally, they can make an announcement to family and friends. Thereafter, they begin purchasing items for the child and celebrating the child's arrival.

The average waiting time for a normal delivery of a baby is 9 months, but it could be, and sometimes is, less than 9 months. The expected parents have a due date to work toward. Finally, they have to be ready to receive the child by making accommodations and preparing for obstacles. Parents must be proactive rather than reactive in raising a child to become a productive, able-bodied adult.

New Beginnings represent your expected baby. You have to take into consideration some of the same factors, just like a couple, when you start your New Beginnings. Ok, you have read all the chapters, followed all the steps, and you are still waiting for something to happen. If you are patient, consistent, and prayerful, you will accomplish your goals in any area (school, work or relationships).

While you are waiting, make sure you are totally prepared for what will happen next. Have you asked yourself the tough questions? What are you willing to accept when the opportunity comes along? What are your standards? Do you want something or someone that will be challenging or agreeable to manage? What will you do if you are presented with two New Beginnings at the same time? In any case, decide on the New Beginnings that will bring you contentment for the rest of your life. Prepare for your New Beginnings physically, emotionally, mentally and financially. When doubt comes along, say to yourself, "I will try my very best to stay on my current path, and I will not give up. I will be patient as I wait to see what God has planned for me."

Continue to wait, stay in prayer, persevere, and keep in touch with the Master Builder (Jesus Christ). When the time is right, when you have matured, when you are prepared, and when you are in continuous prayer, your New Beginnings will start.

Welcome to your New Beginnings! Today is a new day for a new life in Christ and a time for you to live life to the fullest. I know this is a big commitment, and you want to give it your very best, and I believe you can and you will. Just like new parents, you are anxious and encouraged, but you are also nervous about what's to come. You are looking forward to a new experience, new opportunity, new acquaintances, new environments and new procedures. You have prepared your mind with the word from God and with affirmations. You have prepared your environment by removing the junk, trash, negativity, and anything else that might prevent you from reaching your destiny.

You are ready to receive your blessing by making room in your life for new changes.

Some of the changes you will expect and some you will not expect. Just remember, you can make it through by thinking of things that are pure, good and healthy. Stay within the goal of your present budget. You do not want to spend more money than you have earned. Make sure you have health coverage to maintain your well-being. This is your time to flourish and appreciate life.

Celebrate, share with others, and be thankful for New Beginnings, regardless of the size of your accomplishments. "Celebration time, come on..." This is your life. Your accomplishment may not be the first item on your possibilities list, but it is a kickoff to what is to come in your life. Continue to work on the things that matter most to you on your possibilities list. If your New Beginnings prompt you to enroll in a new school, begin a new job, embark on better health regimens, or initiate a new relationship, don't wait until the first day to commence training. If you need to acquire new skills, study immediately. If you will be working with different cultures, take a course in cultural diversity.

You have been given a new opportunity to grow. Learn from your situation, seek options to make the situation better for yourself, and don't drown yourself in feelings of despair ever again. Remember, people and things will come and go in your life. Do not depend on people or things to make you happy. Do not listen to the negative words of others; do only what you want to do with your life. Do not allow other people to define who you are in life. God will always be there; He will never leave. Depend on God.

Life is a journey; you don't stop at New Beginnings. New Beginnings are just that, a time for improving or redirecting the life you are living. You will live life with a fresh new start. You will encounter new adventures, which may lead to new pain and new ways to handle it. There will be other things you will have to accept and/or endure. Sometimes when we face the unknown of the future, we experience fear and we make mistakes. Those mistakes may cause us pain. Don't stress! Look at them as minor setbacks to new possibilities and adjustments to other New Beginnings.

Thank God that we can have more New Beginnings! I cannot count the number of New Beginnings God has allowed me to have in my life. Since New Beginnings are a process, some may find difficulty adjusting to their new way of life. Sometimes you have to take a step backward before you can move forward. Sometimes you have to study and work harder than you have ever worked before in your life. If your New Beginnings are not what you wanted or intended them to be, select another option from your list of possibilities. Remember the blueprint; if you don't like it, select another one. Revisit, regroup, refocus and readjust by reading the previous chapters that relate to your situation. That way, you are better prepared to handle what life throws at you.

If your New Beginnings are everything you prayed for and more, you can revisit your possibilities list and work on the next category (Physiological Needs, Security Needs, Social Needs, Esteem Needs, Self-Actualizing Needs and Medical Needs). Select one goal at a time from your possibilities list. You will be surprised at what you can accomplish. Each victory will bring you closer to winning the battle of life. Bear in mind, your New Beginnings are your "baby". When you give a child the right amount of nourishment, the child will develop into a big, strong and beautiful individual.

Try your very best to master what is needed and give it 110% until the last moment. Become the expert in your field. Recognize when you are out-growing your New Beginnings or becoming bored with them. At this point, evaluate what you are doing and why you want to continue. As previously shown, continue to discover life and all it has to offer, and continue to be blessed by God.

And we know that all things work together for good to those who love God, to those who are the called according to His purpose.
(Romans 8:28)

In conclusion, the key steps to living Life to the Fullest are to love God with all your heart, soul, strength and mind, to love your neighbors as yourself, and to love yourself. Review the chapters in the book for inspiration as you pursue your ultimate reward. Review what you have achieved with the mighty hands of God.

This is the Lord's doing and it is marvelous. You have reached the rainbow, so enjoy the treasures. Don't forget that you hold the keys to your future. Keep this affirmation: "I Won't Give Up...I Want To Live...And Live Life To The Fullest."

I Want to Hear from You!

Don't give up! US small businesses employed 56.8 million people within the last 5 years; there were 115,156,089 private employments in the United States. There are 1,721, two-year colleges, 3,026, four-year colleges, and there are 7 billion people in the world, according to the Bureau of Labor Statistic. Until you have tried every single one of your ideas, you have not tried everything.

I wish you the very best and want you to have the very best for your life. I pray that your life is all that you dreamed; never stop dreaming. I would love to hear from you. Please send me the success stories about your New Beginnings and how this book has blessed your life.

Take the time today to get a copy of this book for someone else so that they too can start living life to the fullest and be blessed.

When you are living in the will of God, when the Bible is your compass, and when God is your father, mother, teacher, counselor and comforter, you are ready for life changing experiences. Let God into your heart and watch all your possibilities come true when you act on His word. Turn to God and run from the devil. God will give you all your desires.

Jesus did not give up when He found His disciples sleeping in the Garden of Gethsemane. Jesus did not give up when Peter denied Him three times, before the rooster crowed once.

Jesus did not give up when He was persecuted, beaten, bruised and crucified on the cross. He allowed himself to die on the cross for our transgressions. Jesus did not give up when He was raised from the dead with all power, so that we would have everlasting life.

You should not give up on Jesus or yourself. Live life to the fullest and be blessed!

You can reach me at:

KayStep1971@gmail.com

or

Kay Stephens
P.O. Box 1254
Red Oak, GA 30272

P.O. Box 453
Powder Springs, Georgia 30127

www.entegritypublishing.com
info@entegritypublishing.com

770.727.6517

CPSIA information can be obtained
at www.ICGtesting.com
Printed in the USA
FSHW020911070519

9 781732 576773